NEW MATH

THE NATIONAL POETRY SERIES

The National Poetry Series was established in 1978 to publish five collections of poetry annually through five participating publishers. The manuscripts are selected by five poets of national reputation. Publication is funded by James A. Michener, Edward J. Piszek, the Copernicus Society of America, the National Endowment for the Arts, the Friends of the National Poetry Series, and the five publishers—E. P. Dutton, Graywolf Press, William Morrow and Company, Persea Books, and the University of Illinois Press.

The National Poetry Series, 1988

The Singing Underneath
  Jeffrey Harrison
  Selected by James Merrill/E. P. Dutton

The Good Thief
  Marie Howe
  Selected by Margaret Atwood/Persea Books

The Hand of God and a Few Bright Flowers
  William Olsen
  Selected by David Wagoner/University of Illinois Press

A Guide to Forgetting
  Jeffrey Skinner
  Selected by Tess Gallagher/Graywolf Press

New Math
  Cole Swensen
  Selected by Michael Palmer/William Morrow and Company

ALSO BY COLE SWENSEN

It's Alive She Says   (Floating Island Publications, 1984)

NEW MATH

Cole Swensen

William Morrow and Company, Inc.

NEW YORK

Grateful acknowledgment is made to the editors of the following magazines in which these poems first appeared:

American Poetry Review, "The Immigrant Carries Her Painting"; *Berkeley Poets Co-Operative*, "Street Scene with Mother and Child"; *Berkeley Poetry Review*, "Simple Test to See If Something's Gone"; *Bottomfish*, "As If All Sound Were Forms of Wind," "Recountable," "Myth," "It's Early Morning All Winter"; *Creeping Bent*, "Grays and Greens"; *Five Fingers Review*, "War on the Past," "Our Town"; *Marin Review*, "All This Time You've Been Driving," "None of the Rain"; *Mariner*, "Harbor," "Secret Ways in Which People Are Free," "After Dark"; *Pavement*, "New Math"; *Poetry London*, "Face"; *Southpaw*, "Argument Against Music," "If Death Were a Matter of Sleeping in the Sea"; *Tempus Fugit*, "Sleep"; *Transfer*, "Plans," "Easy Dreams," "Music for Bars"; *Violent Milk*, "Astonishment Is Killing Me"; *Zyzzyva*, "Fade to Light."

Library of Congress Cataloging-in-Publication Data

Swensen, Cole, 1955–
   New math / Cole Swensen.
     p. cm.
   Poems.
   ISBN 0-688-07869-9
   ISBN 0-688-07968-7 (pbk.)
   I. Title.
PS3569.W384N4   1988b
811'.54—dc19   87-35946
                                         CIP

Printed in the United States of America

First Edition

1 2 3 4 5 6 7 8 9 10

BOOK DESIGN BY KATHLEEN CAREY

This book is dedicated to

PAT AND CHUCK AND LYNN

Contents

"and all that is, lives"

The Immigrant Carries Her Painting

Let me get this picture straight—
the slow gray suface
of a lake that
can't be mistaken
at this angle
her face almost
speaks but a hand
goes up to hold
the mouth on instead
you see she knew
all along, the wharf
would be empty,
her four children standing
there hungry. There is a country
we come to own by leaving.
Later, evening may be the only
way we have of proving it's there.

Through Eyes

like the leopard's
all black
through distance
in the distance
antelope
look like the flames
one will soon become
in his veins.
And if a calm machinery
sharpens, shoulders
firing themselves like shot
and the one thing
this leopard's never figured out:
How this deer
floats up to him,
how his own reflection disappears
out the back of its eye.

Secret Ways in Which People Are Free

Recurrent images

Man in a park, arms outstretched
lined with pigeons etc.

(but you I love only
because you're beautiful,
in itself
a noble thing.)

A stranger wakes up saying
As a child you were afraid of me.

A man flying a kite after dark.

It's Early Morning All Winter

I look at my own
unsent letter. If nothing
could change all winter long.

The strong sound
that leaps off an ax,
such a spider web in the glass air.

Trees step backward,
hands raised, they
too will escape

On a curving line
along a scratch in space
waiting for the light to change.

Street Scene with Mother and Child

You must, and in
turning, slowly
a word sears
the tongue and
run on. Hurry
There is a child
on fire in the street and
lovely. Again slowly.
To laugh like that
is flaming. And her mother,
dying of curiosity,
dresses the perfect body
every morning, even more
miniature hands.
And every morning
like a coin burning
through the back of the sky, naked
she is blue and almost
frightening. And in turn,
hurry.

Easy Dreams

Follow these gloves
All flight is home
Fine delineation
favors one.

Fire as a flavor
beckoning then
The trace of an angle
closing to wind.

To have simply died early
like a taste on your lips
The bracelets conversing
among themselves.
The white fingertips.

New Math

As if the word everything
meant everything
as all words do.
We refer again to prosopognosia*—
that condition in which
the victim cannot distinguish
between faces.
If we could compute the numerical value
of a turning wrist, a sense of shock,
toast on a plate,
paint by number
one picture in a single dimension.
Both portrait and landscape
can trace their ancestry
back to the point.
If every breath
is a separate equation
and yet they all equal zero,
that egg with a vacuum inside,
the insensible which we
sense and call invisible
has succeeded in imaging a new circle,
imagine
any thing in which
each point lies the same
distance from every other.

*The word *prosopognosia* is taken from *Left Brain, Right Brain* by Sally P. Springer and Georg Deutsch (W. H. Freeman, 1981). It is the name of a specific type of aphasia—the inability to recognize faces.

War on the Past

Love is just a clue.

If we win the world
can come back
to the world, speechless

aligned, cell within cell

You must put the objects
down on the table
and walk casually from the room
you cannot re-enter

until we get it right.

All This Time You've Been Driving

The rain is not
falling rather
we are rushing up to it
Translucent wingless insects
vanish into the thought
The night grinding backward
overhead swallow slow
the black honey
flows through you a road
that keeps moving
as later we're reading
or talking or asleep.

Recountable

Indicates discrete units
like days with end.
The simple line,
framable.
All that an eye retains,
simple lines, branches,
flying objects identify the sky.
See how we end as simply as skin.
The percentage of beauty
that is disbelief,
something sideways receiving
all our lives
contain of us, the
simple spine
leaves.

Crowd Scenes

Through the many gathered
someone walks
with carefully measured steps.
Someone is counting

Those who separate the body

Find the numberless eyes
in every cell.

The rain that makes all
leaves one
along the street.

Each cell offers
the perfect replica.

The storming of the Bastille.
The migration of the Monarch butterfly.
The relocation of a tribe
of which all but 100 died.

How many times must you see
a face before you think
you've seen it all your life

Someone walks onward and
the footsteps land inside your wrist.

Our Town

They who had just
put her on the Greyhound bus
leaned on a parked car,
he tapping his fingers
on the roof like they were wondering
what to do with their lives.
A body should be buried
alongside its obsessions:
travel, weather or this
new longing for arrows.
What was never asked for
or had something to fight.
A half a million people
live among the tombstones
of Cairo's largest cemetery.
The setting sun replaces
a few windows in Oakland.
The worlds nobody takes
are inhabited only by hands
and at that, just the palms
in a curved position.

Sleep Like a Kiss

Sleep is astonished smoke
curling back
toward animals
whose eyes flash green
from the light of an oncoming world—
a much rarer mineral than we
have been led to believe,
before your eyes,
sound gilded with nerve endings.
A coin dropped in a dream.
Animals with dates on their hooves.
That so much should pass
in a shadow without an object.
A kiss like a laugh
that never meets the air.

Background

God is a color,
gray and green mixed
with equal parts water.
Stones turn to stone
in the winter everything
joins the river. This is why
I live here: creek,
stream, canal and alder.
Later I'll dissolve within the picture;
some thicker syllable of laughter
or a long aching whistle
past the bend in the weather.
The memory will appear
slightly sharper.

An Argument Against Music

Guess lost

something long becoming
paved before the chance

You know we would have returned
quietly to our homes.

There was no need to prove it.

He with a suitcase in every pocket
and that body in the river
without life now can sigh

"Let me take you
to my family"

Let my shirts
stream out far behind me

Let you hum this tune
when you are thinking of nothing.

And the one man rose
and the other man ran.

You see no less with the eyes closed.
The picture lights itself
on fire in the street.
The flow of water is accidentally graceful.
Sometimes you don't notice you're humming
until someone asks you to stop.

For the Duration

Black and white
as is always;
the news. The face
within the fear.
It was still cool
with morning. He was
thinking of something
else at the time. In open hands
lay open hands.
(The knife covered with tears.)
"Lately I see my work
first in white, many
many shades of it."
"I looked back and
the whole city
was in flames." A single
mast of smoke
light as salt.
There is no end to the New World.
There is a fuzzy picture
on the front page of the paper
every morning
I am stopped by the shock,
this time it was you.

As If All Sound Were Forms of Wind

Does a leaf moving
through air create a sound
or is it the sound of
leaves, things against
each other. Or does
the air groan as it's dismembered.

The hand which is
much older now
is writing about the sun.
A leaf placed in orbit.
How of course fire
was thought a god.

I think air groans as it's dismembered
or a ship is assembling
itself beyond the dark.

Cathedral

A rural man with a common name
A gap in our memory
The sound of a chisel into stone
still falling deeper into it.

It was there in his hands
the whole time. The key
and the pointed arch,
the waking early
and the lack of math.

No, in the lines of the palm
are those of the temple, know
the angles of a lover yawning
let in light which for all
its speed may never land.

It took him centuries
to knead out the weight
until they floated
from his hands at the final cut.

This is the hush that dissolves the service,
the forgetful air to the congregation.

He went to work every morning
like every other man,
uphill without end

but someone got to place the finishing piece
and shrink to a sound as he stood below. Amiens.
Ascent without boundaries
and with so much history to go.
When we dream we dream alone,
the only true flight is that of stone.

Falling in Spherical Silence

A hand,
a refraction of dreaming,
wanders into mine
not callous,
not conscious
not off-hand

In the simplest world
of numbers nothing
is indivisible
and this cannot
occur to me

This one too, is
a machine, it can be
reduced to nonmoving parts.

But the bodies sway like separate lightning

And the arm too,
is dreaming and
everything below the mind
slips like tide
through branches

Perhaps you believe even less
in the physical world

And I envy the air
its apparent homogeniety,
bodies mixed so evenly
they disappear.

Lullaby

A small black book
way out on the ocean,
break my world in two.
The violent seams,
preferable orbits,
a boat pulls up
like evening and
drives you half to sleep.
All across the universe,
incredible speed.
The world that ends
is already in your hands,
or a spot washed out of the sea.

Work in Progress: Dusk

Because there is a band playing
in the park the people linger
so their children keep on running,
charcoal smudges going
deeper into the paper
disappearing into the fur
of the dark and then
emerging. Small druids
in their bodies whenever
their parents aren't watching.
No, just smudges growing
arms and running closer
the way form spreads across canvas
even while the painter is watching.

Grays and Greens

We have found there are thousands
separable with tweezers
like oak leaves after rain
are individually wrapped in shellac.
Cold salt like sunlight shaking
down through fog. Each god drives
a different car through your hair.
The forest on its long walk
into landscape, sheep on a hillside
as if something living could also move.

No Worry

No, worry about nothing
but the chiseling
of hills into distance
in the slight haze

and sleep lost over color
no two ever the same

the wringing hands
float ashore amazed.
Worry about beauty.
It can sell you anything.
Lakes collect in the
chambers of the heart
where the sailboats are made
of flying fish about
the size of match heads.

Sleep can be lost as
easily as a house key,
the shock can consume
at any moment
if the hills are not rising
weather is wearing them down
and you are driving
north in the late afternoon
or holding your eyes
in your hands like addresses.

Saffron Pickers Under a Dead Blue Sky

Dead as in absolute,
no incursions of shadow,
no stations to the sun,
but everything that fingers touch
has to be retold.
Here the light builds up in drifts
and the workers,
their hands stained with it,
blend.

A Simple Test to See If Something's Gone

If you went to touch it right now
could you? Time passes differently
through different rooms.
The object either is there
or is not
based on available light.
Today merely repeats the pattern.
In the still, warm jar of an hour
evening parachutes upward.
However they say
if you just squeeze your hands
together hard enough
with your fingertips wired
to a certain part of your brain.

Except That She Remembered

Not naming a face,
just a name.

Asked to believe that something
has happened here.

Pursued by the assumption:
objects have no memory

neither do hands until
you look at them.

Look at them:
they act as though nothing
disappears. They act as though
they were not there

but here, falling through space
with the great leaves of darkness.

And she never said a word
and the fragments this will bloom within

the glass windowsills
with versions suspended inside

and inside the picture
imitating a closed universe

in which we must someday
be her again.

Topographical Map of the Sky

A sudden curve
inside the sight
gleam, then turn
it turns away.

Glance that burns
but knows its course.
The hinted eye
a throat of light.

Blueprint lit
inside a wave,
orbit form,
it settles clear.

The figure traced
in motion splayed,
objects that comprise
a day

deeper yet
more carefully stored,
the twist of thought
and its spiral key.

Myth

Only the horns of
the great animal remain
charging. And the
streetcar full
of single passengers.
How well we know
the neighborhood.
The barricade of light
screaming for home.
The time it takes
to turn and run.
How you will sit in
the quiet of an evening
and create it.
A marvelous beast
crashes through backyards,
electricity in the fields,
along the smallest
hairs of the body.

You Pass a Man on the Street

You pass a man on the street
and years later lose an hour distracted
because you picture but can't place him.

What do colors do
in their private lives?

Everything in the world
means the world to me
and I find this to be
mathematically correct.

You pass a man on the street
and don't even see him.
You do this every day of your life.

Color is broken light.

Plans

That it should come in pieces
like mail,
the history
of a similar world.
What does it matter
if a stranger is lying?
Impossible you say,
this too is your life,
this tendency of matter
to proceed toward disorder.
This knife held up to the sun
gets mistaken for the time of day.
The line that by its end
is sleep. Make it equal zero.

Never Dream When You're Hungry

Under a microscope it seems
armed with uncountable hands.
The minutes in their elliptical orbits
spinning away.
Discussing what
could have been, what with all
the shining pieces and the bone,
was done.

Downtown

A member of the museum.
A tree pruned to a moving object.
This is outside.
(Later that night returning
heels crack on concrete.
All the ghosts)
are frozen in their stalls.
And in the words of another
other countries that look
just like this.
Light stratified
to resemble memory.
A salesman on the street.
A mailbox.
The nature of verbs in this language
does not automatically distinguish
between day and night.
The number of children.
The familiarity of stone.

Music for Bars

Undifferentiated memory.
"I think you'll have a
hard time proving it."
In the background
a game of pool
clean as scissors.
It's a specific sound
and you shudder but it
pleases you.

A Long Story

There must have been two people.
If light travels over
1,000 miles to strike a face.
A core sample of
undeveloped film reveals
weather patterns unseen
by the naked eye.
I guess they loved each other.
An address divisible
by only itself and one.
Each race stores its history
in the shadows its occupants
cast at midday.
Layer upon layer.
They must have lived forever
but under assumed names.
Among the travelers of every nation
passes the seed
of a fixed place.
Layer after layer
disclosed the same face.
I guess they've found traces
of where we walk at night.

After Dark

A cigarette burning
in an empty house.

Where do they go at night
among the flying hands?

An oar bites deep into
the atmosphere then disappears.

And all the dead
are the same one.

Astonishment Is Killing Me

Astonishment is killing me,
how many numbers are there
or is there only more than one.
And no the hand is not
quicker than the eye,
it's something else
you're hearing for I've
turned the radio off
she said, turning
but in such a rhythm as to
blend in with the other
objects in the room.
I too have been cut
from a magazine without waking
dream is transformed by matches
into the term "shocked"
by the thousand muscles
that interlock to turn a page
into the lungs of this room.
Breath is an oar
by which we see
a line of small boats leaving,

your simplicity is killing me,
you add aloud in your sleep.

Changing Lanes

requires an immense equation.
The horse has switched
riders in middream.
Not to see an unidentified object
hanging in the path.
I am remembering the day for you.
Out of several boxes lined with doubt
there is bound to come
a lock of hair.
Tie a good knot,
the horse will bolt
at the approach of a stranger,
by tomorrow you will
no longer be in the photograph.

Later

So tired rain completely
engaging
are gears how the sky
stripped blue
paint is an eyelid
you are a believer
This intricate weather
codes a shatter of traveling
braille wing around
two tired people completely
entertained by the rain.

Sleep

The ocean, like any storm,
has an eye
where you can sleep
to the sound,
hundreds of miles away,
of languages,
of the end of the world,

of whole civilizations
that dream as animals,
holographically perfect,
the sky as big as floating
on your back down a river

you can't describe
without the words
forming in your throat
the distance within which
a body can see itself;

a loud sound in the night
that wakes you with a start
and fearing thieves.

Still Dusk

Three days later
it was summer,
air saying nothing on the skin,
hills; a jury hung with light
on tongues saying nothing.
Here is the reflection
off the lake
off which the sheets
have just been drawn,
a light in early summer travels
backward from dawn.

Harbor

Some nights the sea
is so still
the image doesn't flinch.

Oil on the surface,
the other boats
in lines

and the oil catches
the moon
in its rearview mirror
and shudders.

See, I have packed the air
with the scent
you cannot become

any more real
by awakening
in the morning.

Other Lives by Other Rivers

Figures, recurrent
kneeling like window shades
over and over clutching
the weather to their solutions
flickering like water

That time of day

Expressed as music
you would feel only
your bones falling
and gravity deciding
to stray

The past is water soluble
The figure is an atmospheric condition
You couldn't paint it if you tried
I dreamt myself to death last time
The window opened
like a fist into a palm

The window opened
and the figure rose
and the river fell
from her shoulders
to earth. Other
explanations have been offered

but we confused
the moment with music
She drowned with her
mouth open and each
note equally suspended

The boats hovering like dreams
occurring in split seconds
The drifting stays on your hands
for days. Constellations begin
to look like the things they're named for.

None of the Rain

Perhaps it is the same
precise water
after traveling
now rattling its beads.
Fingertips all on their own.

And none of the rain
comes in through the open window.

The migration selects
an inner eye,
and there in the background,
water gifted with sight.
It gazes in at another world
in which a mirror hangs
on the opposite wall in which
rain is something containable.

As If Death Were a Matter of Sleeping in the Sea

One if part is breaking
Mast ahead the danger might
Another chance be taking him
Cloud cover. Literal dream.
Real hands this time.

Leaving the House

The crowd of your voice,
both the mouth of and the river.
What we remember walks backward
tearing off doors.
Flood. But what was it that you said?
The photographs are growing flames.
The rooms are lined with boxes.
We are being moved.
It's almost like listening to music.

The Man Who Slept with the Wind

This is a story of darkness
and sounds that mean nothing
more than what you see.
The dead hold up the earth
by breathing deeply
and wind can be made
to tell what it hears,
the minor structural differences
between the earth and the past.
This is the story he was telling when
you fell asleep you erased the end.

A Grandfather

Dead now.
Before I was born.
A suicide.
How cliché.
You knew him did you?
Pass the gravy please.
Silent like a cellar,
wearing silence like a skin.
But you knew.
What he wouldn't say
(before I was born)
did you write it down?
Shh. The others
will be back soon.
And each of you
claims to be the only
one who knew?
No.
You are wrong.
It is me
he speaks to.

Something You Said

Light being a device for lifting.
Something on the stair. Blank.
"If I blink three times,"

The odd remarks, the
rubbed out sky,

all your voices,
particles of harbor,
some further breakdown,
"No, not at all like that."

A stream of simple observations,
leaves, things below heels.
You said something about dusting.
You said something about dust.

Something light, maybe paper
has fallen to the floor.
Punctuation of background noises,
traffic perhaps or sunlight on the stair,

voices follow us, satellites
and as such are always falling
in so permanent a way that
it looks intentional.

Even as you sit here with me
your words return, calling.

Light, When Sleeping

Glaze
It could have been a face
instead of caught
within marble these thousands of years

To open an egg
and find it there lying
with all the time
that falls off a naked body
in piles nearby a chip of it

cut out and placed
open in the doorway
a silence that is
the eye of speed.

Time and the Animals

Approximate flight

The flickering home
set with hooves
cutting moons seconds long
into the earth as brief

Speaking of the lion,
the pain is equally good to him,
the spear-shaped blood
discarding direction

It's all this filling,
language without consonants,
the edges falling off
of things left and right.

What Flight Will Be Like

The river's muscle
laughing itself to death.
I leaned on my elbow
(laughter in a dark room)
and watched the crowd passing,
millions of separate pieces
simultaneously forgetting everything.
I rise and leave the building.
"If you dig deep enough
you'll get to China."
A balloon explodes
just behind me to the left
and I freeze for an instant.

Face

What in a face speaks the record
that the mouth, word by word,
forgets? Recognition
rings in the blood
and it is this, this intravenous kind of surety
with which your face reoccurs, reoccurs,
it is perfect; I have checked this
and I have watched your hands,
your actions in detail, in dimly lit rooms
your face alone
is visible.
It is the only perfection for miles
the opening wing of your face
casts a shadow

and this face has come to haunt me;
perhaps I am walking home
past the wharves, it follows.
I have ceased to mind its presence.
I strain and try to hear it.
There is a thin, thin sound
coming from the boathouses
where the watchlights almost reach
one another across the shadows.
A movement under the eaves
catches my eye; at a glance

I think it is your face I see
but going closer, no, dozens
of moths are splintering their cocoons,
a fine dust is falling
over everything.

The Seven Wonders of the Future World

for B.N.

At some point we'll start
all being born
with the same face.

Darkness
will acquire the texture
of fur and will be
all the grief we need.

Stars will be replaced
by spiders creating
lightning storms as they
spin, laughter will be
recognized and accepted
as the universal language.

All objects will become
either a saxophone or a drum.

You will breathe again.

In utter calm that yet
includes a storm,
blue as deep as the moment
weather destroys its keys.

The word "we" will become singular.

Re

The planet white in the distance,
a single stroke and it's gone.
And overheard music
and the rest of it,
undone aligned with unborn.
The slow curve of decision
all the way down the optical nerve.
An instant lit in passing
that retains a light inside.
You know those shades of blue
that illuminate highways—
love is not a transitive verb.

Song Without Music

Of the many times
I've been married
I remember you
a house
a window
facing south.
What was it our child saw there?
Of all the times
I've been married
I'll never speak a word,
so the windmill says,
let the sky turn
and the earth be still;
you are all I know of learning.
Let the sun turn
so that the earth will
ask us to sleep with her
tonight you are all
I know a window
faces east in dream,
north in midsummer,
was it our child we saw there?
pacing before it
until winter moaned
and the sky turned brilliant green.
The first time I married you
I cried myself to sleep.

I thought you said
the earth was burning.
The first time I married
was on a quiet street.
That silence has never quit returning.
Was it a child we saw there?
It goes on like this, unwinding.

Not Necessarily Bone

That at the center of the sun
a simple film
Something blooms, easy
The turning of ships,
the weather
there

are 17 ladders attached to the eye
but it's useless

Though wonder is not relative
The ever of how
And the length of the eclipse
has come to live inside.

Fade to Light

Hand me this hand
The sail is bent
The trail is sold
and the wind tied in knots

Answer the phone
The tune is left
The stones uncoil
in a wide-angle lens

A search for clues
encounters bliss
A lip on the edge
of the flowering dark

A shell falls with hail
Hidden and hides
The following sky
The descending kiss.

Born in San Francisco in 1955, Cole Swensen received a B.A. and M.A. in English/creative writing from San Francisco State University, where she was subsequently a lecturer in creative writing. She also taught for seven years with the California Poets in the Schools program, and from 1985 to 1987 was director of the Marin Poetry Center. She is the recipient of a Creative Advancement Grant from the Marin Arts Council, and lives in northern California.